The *Little Book* of

SNOWFLAKES

by Kenneth Libbrecht

Voyageur Press

Edited by Kari Cornell
Designed by Maria Friedrich
Printed in China

04 05 06 07 08   5 4 3 2 1

Library of Congress Cataloging-in-
Publication Data

Libbrecht, Kenneth George.
  The little book of snowflakes / by
Kenneth Libbrecht
      p. cm.
  ISBN 0-89658-652-9 (hardcover)
  1. Snowflakes—Pictorial works. I. Title
    QC926.36.L53 2004
      551.57'841—dc22
                        2004009378

Distributed in Canada by Raincoast
Books, 9050 Shaughnessy Street,
Vancouver, B.C. V6P 6E5

Published by Voyageur Press, Inc.
123 North Second Street, P.O. Box 338,
Stillwater, MN 55082 U.S.A.
651-430-2210, fax 651-430-2211
books@voyageurpress.com
www.voyageurpress.com

**Educators, fundraisers, premium and gift
buyers, publicists, and marketing managers:**
Looking for creative products and new
sales ideas? Voyageur Press books are
available at special discounts when
purchased in quantities, and special
editions can be created to your
specifications. For details contact the
marketing department at 800-888-9653.

OUT OF THE BOSOM OF THE AIR

OUT OF THE CLOUD-FOLDS OF HER GARMENTS SHAKEN,

OVER THE WOODLANDS BROWN AND BARE,

OVER THE HARVEST-FIELDS FORSAKEN,

SILENT, AND SOFT, AND SLOW

DESCENDS THE SNOW.

—Henry Wadsworth Longfellow (1807–1882)

The images in this book are of freshly fallen snowflakes, captured using a special photo-microscope. The most symmetrical crystals are usually found during light snowfalls, with little wind, when the weather is especially cold.

THOSE WHO DWELL AMONG THE BEAUTIES AND MYSTERIES
OF THE EARTH ARE NEVER ALONE OR WEARY OF LIFE.
—Rachel Carson (1907–64)

SIMPLE PLEASURES ARE THE LAST HEALTHY REFUGE
IN A COMPLEX WORLD.

—Oscar Wilde (1854-1900)

You need very little to enjoy the rich beauty of snowflakes—just an inexpensive magnifier, a light snowfall, and a curious eye.

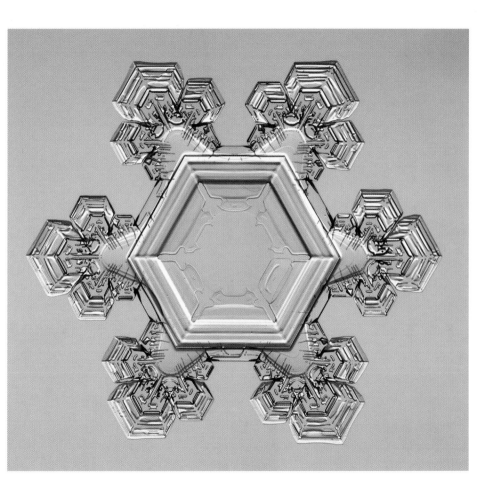

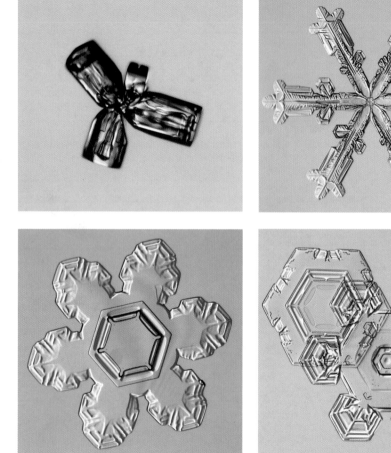

Many well-formed snowflakes have six nearly symmetrical branches. Sometimes you may find twelve-branched snowflakes as well. One thing you will not find falling from the sky is an eight-sided snowflake.

> JOY IN LOOKING AND COMPREHENDING IS NATURE'S
> MOST BEAUTIFUL GIFT.
>
> —Albert Einstein (1879–1955)

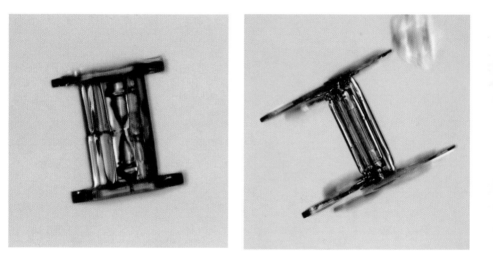

A capped column forms in a two-step process. Initially the crystal grows as a stubby column, but then the wind carries it to a colder location, causing thin plates to develop on each end.

IF THE LORD ALMIGHTY HAD CONSULTED ME BEFORE
EMBARKING ON CREATION, I SHOULD HAVE RECOMMENDED
SOMETHING SIMPLER.

—Alphonso the Wise (1221–1289)

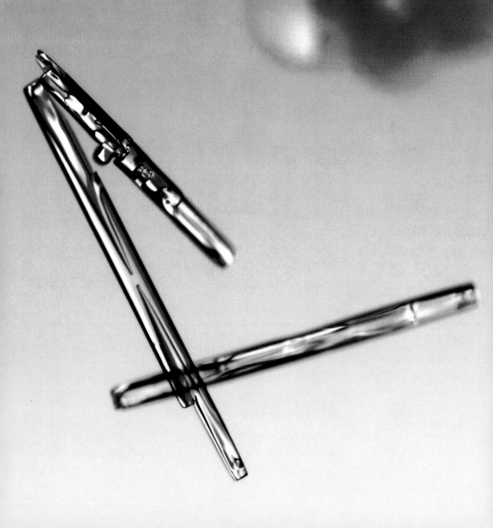

No other substance grows in such a fascinating variety of crystalline forms as ice. Depending on weather conditions, snowflakes can grow into slender needles, thick columns, thin plates, multibranched stars, or countless other intriguing shapes.

A symmetrical snowflake is not a frozen raindrop, but rather a
single crystal of ice that grows directly from water vapor in the air.
The process takes about fifteen minutes, as the snowflake slowly
drifts to earth.

THIS GRAND SHOW IS ETERNAL. IT IS ALWAYS SUNRISE
SOMEWHERE: THE DEW IS NEVER ALL DRIED AT ONCE; A
SHOWER IS FOREVER FALLING; VAPOR EVER RISING.
ETERNAL SUNRISE, ETERNAL SUNSET, ETERNAL DAWN AND
GLOAMING, ON SEAS AND CONTINENTS AND ISLANDS.
EACH IN ITS TURN, AS THE ROUND EARTH ROLLS.

   —John Muir (1838–1914)

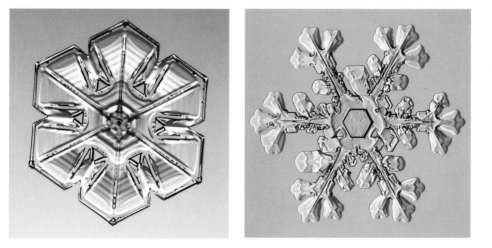

We do not yet understand all the subtle mysteries of snowflakes.
Exactly how the simple interactions of water molecules produce
such a dramatic diversity of structures remains a puzzle.

NATURE WILL BEAR THE CLOSEST INSPECTION. SHE INVITES US TO LAY OUR EYE LEVEL WITH HER SMALLEST LEAF, AND TAKE AN INSECT VIEW OF ITS PLAIN.

—Henry David Thoreau (1817–1862)

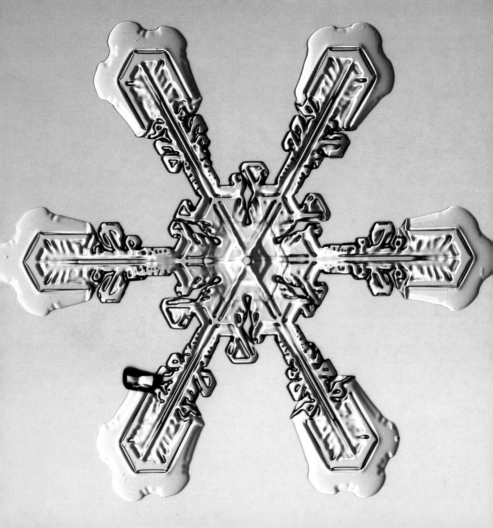

IN ALL THINGS OF NATURE THERE IS SOMETHING OF THE MARVELOUS.

—Aristotle (384 BC–322 BC)

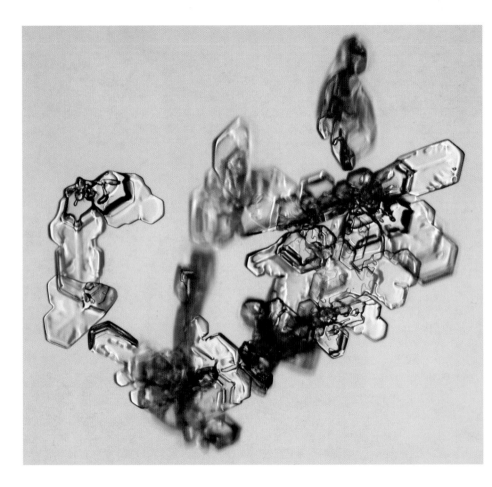

COMMONLY THE FLAKES REACH US TRAVEL-WORN AND AGGLOMERATED, COMPARATIVELY WITHOUT ORDER OR BEAUTY, FAR DOWN IN THEIR FALL, LIKE MEN IN THEIR ADVANCED AGE.

— Henry David Thoreau (1817–1862)

Well-formed, symmetrical snowflakes are the exception, not the rule. Snow usually falls in agglomerations of small crystal fragments, like cold, fluffy sand.

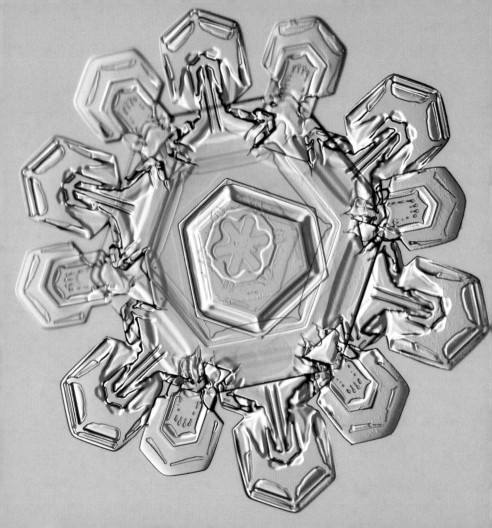

If you look carefully, you're likely to find some *double stars* falling
from the sky. These appear when two six-branched crystals form
together, joined at the center.

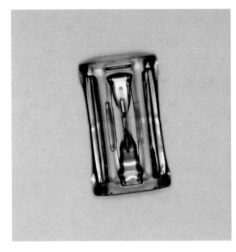

IF NATURE WERE NOT BEAUTIFUL, IT WOULD NOT BE WORTH KNOWING, AND IF NATURE WERE NOT WORTH KNOWING, LIFE WOULD NOT BE WORTH LIVING.

—Henri Poincaré (1854–1912)

BESIDES COMBINING HER GREATEST SKILL AND ARTISTRY
IN THE PRODUCTION OF SNOWFLAKES, NATURE GENER-
OUSLY FASHIONS THE MOST BEAUTIFUL SPECIMENS ON A
VERY THIN PLANE SO THAT THEY ARE SPECIALLY ADAPTED
FOR PHOTOMICROGRAPHICAL STUDY.

—Wilson Bentley (1865–1931)

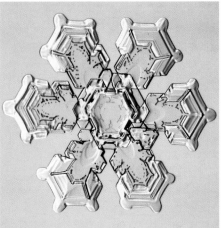

To see a World in a grain of Sand,
And a Heaven in a Wild Flower,
Hold Infinity in the palm of your hand,
And Eternity in an hour.

—William Blake (1757–1827)

On its journey through the clouds, a snowflake will often collide with numerous cloud droplets, called rime.

THERE IS A PLEASURE IN THE PATHLESS WOODS,

THERE IS A RAPTURE ON THE LONELY SHORE,

THERE IS A SOCIETY WHERE NONE INTRUDES,

BY THE·DEEP SEA AND MUSIC IN ITS ROAR:

I LOVE NOT MAN THE LESS, BUT NATURE MORE.

—Lord Byron (1788–1824)

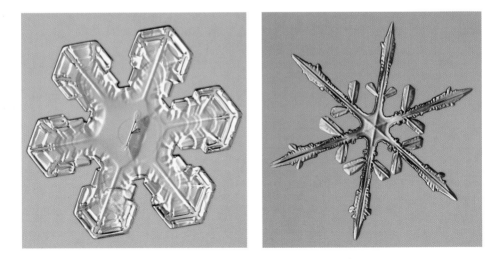

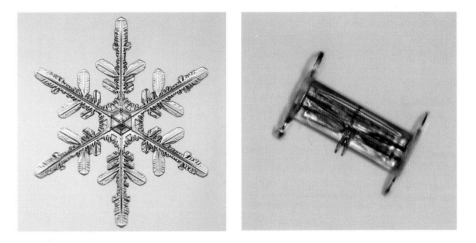

Different snowfalls bring different types of snowflakes. Needles and columns are frequent in warmer weather; stellar crystals appear at lower temperatures. Often the forms change from one hour to the next, as the cloud conditions change.

THE RUDDY CLOUDS FLOAT IN THE FOUR QUARTERS OF
THE CERULEAN SKY. AND THE WHITE SNOWFLAKES SHOW
FORTH THEIR SIX-PETALED FLOWERS.

—Hsiao Tung, sixth century scholar

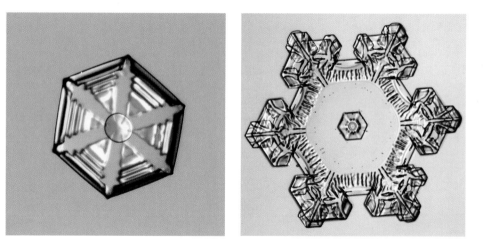

The six-fold symmetry of a snowflake ultimately derives from the geometry of the water molecules from which it is made. The molecules hook together to form a hexagonal structure, and this construction affects the overall growth of the crystal.

Stellar dendrites are large snowflakes with a multibranched, almost plantlike appearance.

Many snow crystals are delineated by ridges, forming what are called sectored plates.

WHOSE WOODS THESE ARE I THINK I KNOW.
HIS HOUSE IS IN THE VILLAGE THOUGH;
HE WILL NOT SEE ME STOPPING HERE
TO WATCH HIS WOODS FILL UP WITH SNOW.
—Robert Frost (1874–1963)

THE PURSUIT OF TRUTH AND BEAUTY IS A SPHERE OF
ACTIVITY IN WHICH WE ARE PERMITTED TO REMAIN
CHILDREN ALL OUR LIVES.

—Albert Einstein (1879-1955)

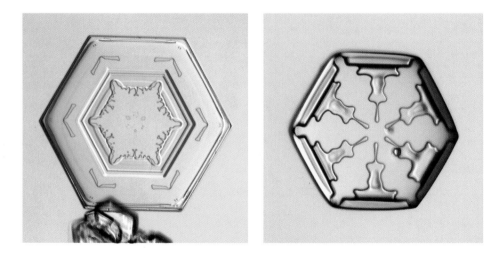

It would seem that nature cannot be content in producing a plain
snowflake. Even the simplest hexagon of ice, no larger than the
head of a pin, must be decorated with its own unique pattern.

HOW FULL OF THE CREATIVE GENIUS IS THE AIR IN WHICH THESE ARE GENERATED! I SHOULD HARDLY ADMIRE MORE IF REAL STARS FELL AND LODGED ON MY COAT. NATURE IS FULL OF GENIUS, FULL OF THE DIVINITY; SO THAT NOT A SNOWFLAKE ESCAPES ITS FASHIONING HAND.

—Henry David Thoreau (1817–1862)

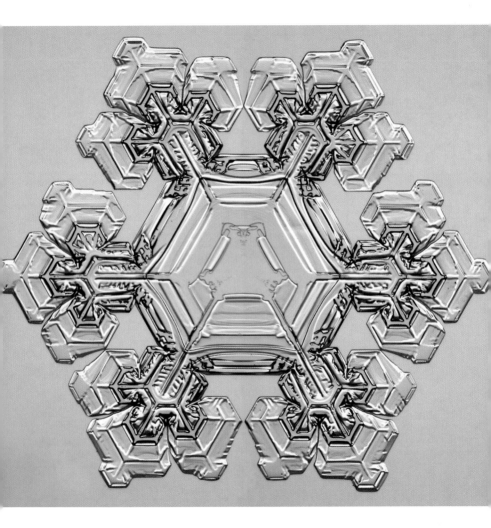

NATURE IS EVER AT WORK BUILDING AND PULLING DOWN, CREATING AND DESTROYING, KEEPING EVERYTHING WHIRLING AND FLOWING, ALLOWING NO REST BUT IN RHYTHMICAL MOTION, CHASING EVERYTHING IN ENDLESS SONG OUT OF ONE BEAUTIFUL FORM INTO ANOTHER.

— John Muir (1838–1914)

A cloud is made from countless microscopic water droplets.
When a cloud freezes, snowflakes result.

NEVER MAKE ANYTHING SIMPLE AND
EFFICIENT WHEN A WAY CAN BE FOUND
TO MAKE IT COMPLEX AND WONDERFUL.
　　—Unknown

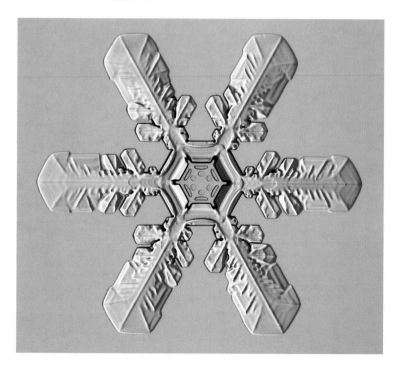

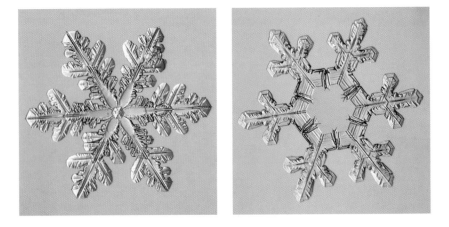

Snowflakes form complex shapes because ice crystal growth is
extremely sensitive to temperature and humidity. Simply moving
from place to place within a cloud is sufficient to produce a
near-infinite variety of different snowflake patterns.

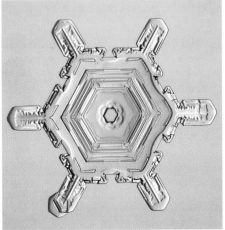

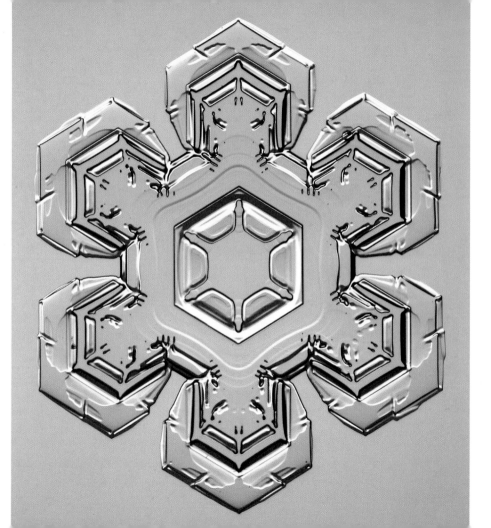

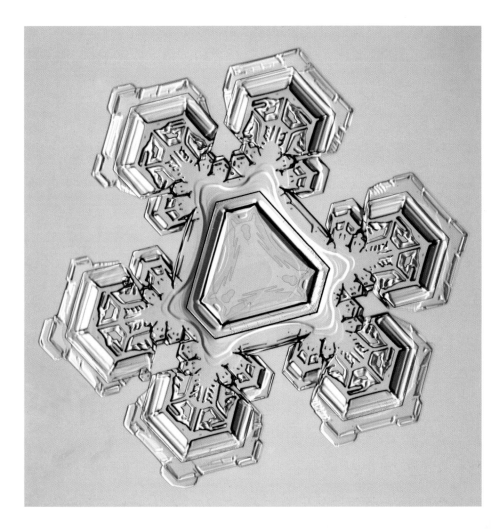

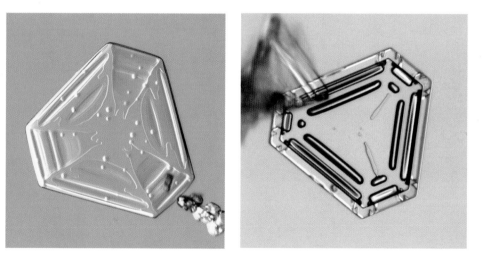

Snowflakes can sometimes be found with three-fold symmetry,
although this is rare.

IF I HAD INFLUENCE WITH THE GOOD FAIRY WHO IS
SUPPOSED TO PRESIDE OVER THE CHRISTENING OF ALL
CHILDREN, I SHOULD ASK THAT HER GIFT TO EACH CHILD
IN THE WORLD BE A SENSE OF WONDER SO INDESTRUC-
TIBLE THAT IT WOULD LAST THROUGHOUT LIFE.

—Rachel Carson (1907-64)

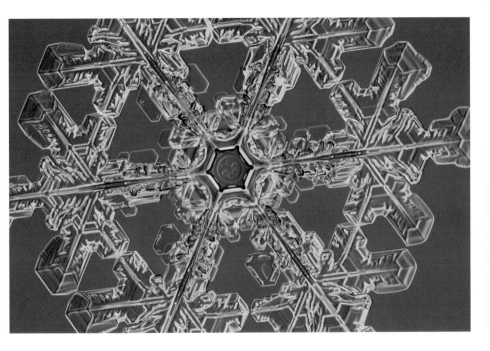

Snowflakes, being made of ice, are clear and colorless. By using lighting of different colors, however, a photographer can achieve a variety of rainbow effects.

THE CHIEF FORMS OF BEAUTY ARE ORDER
AND SYMMETRY AND DEFINITENESS.
—Aristotle (384 BC–322 BC)

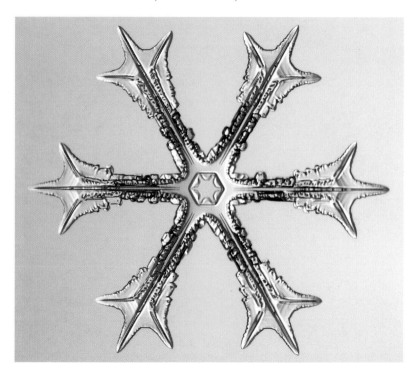

There is no blueprint that guides the construction of a snowflake;
its pattern emerges as it tumbles through the clouds.

THERE IS NOTHING IN THE WORLD MORE BEAUTIFUL THAN THE FOREST CLOTHED TO ITS VERY HOLLOWS IN SNOW. IT IS THE STILL ECSTASY OF NATURE, WHEREIN EVERY SPRAY, EVERY BLADE OF GRASS, EVERY SPIRE OF REED, EVERY INTRICACY OF TWIG, IS CLAD WITH RADIANCE.

—Fiona Macleod (1855–1905)

The author, with his traveling snowflake photomicroscope, in search of the perfect snowflake. (photo by Rachel Wing)